the 'author's secrets' series

Writing

Tips and Tricks

More Than 40 Ways to Improve YOUR Writing Today!

kim lambert

Dreamstone Publishing © 2015

www.dreamstonepublishing.com

2nd edition

ISBN:

ISBN-13:   978-1-925165-72-2

Disclaimer

All writing is an experiment in a sense, and many people come to the same or similar ideas over time. Each person expresses their ideas, and describes how they work slightly differently – our ideas and approaches come in our own personal 'voice'. All writing tips in this book have been derived from the author's personal experience, and that of other authors that she has coached and worked with. Should any bear a close resemblance to those used elsewhere, that is purely coincidental.

If you would like to provide feedback on this book please send it to info@dreamstonepublishing.com

Other Books in the "Author's Secrets" Series

Watch out for

"How to Write – Right Now"

coming soon!

Thank You For Buying This Book !

I hope that you enjoy it (and the many amazing stories, books, blog posts or articles that you write, using these tips).

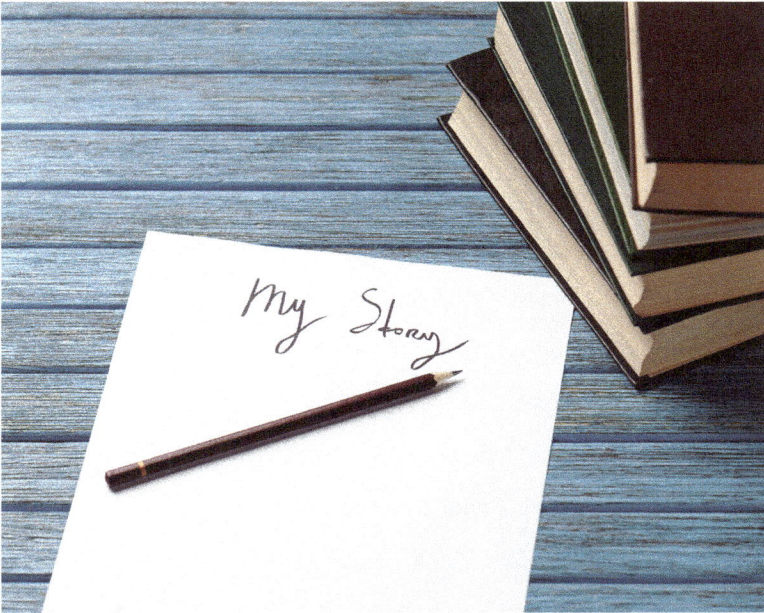

Please leave me a review on Amazon and let us, and other readers, know what you think!

Table of Contents

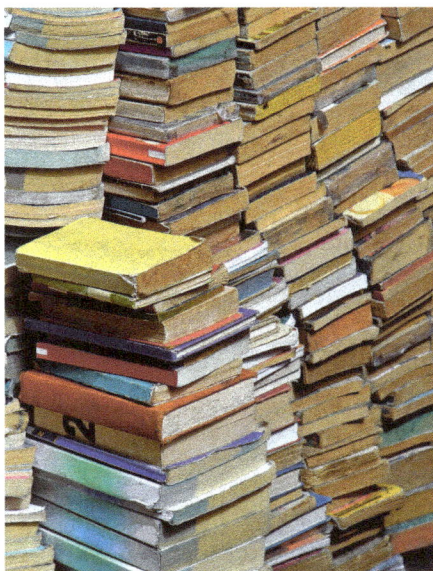

What Readers are Saying About This Book

◆

"What a perfect book for upcoming Authors, and even current Authors! This book provides quality tips and questions that will encourage any writer to create their own unique piece of literature! It's set out so simply, and easy to read – and is FULL of everything a writer needs to know!

A *'must have'* for anyone who wants to turn that dream of writing a book – into a reality!"

Di McMath, Amazon Bestselling Author of
"Icebreakers: How to Empower, Motivate and Inspire Your Team, Through Step-by-Step Activities That Boost Confidence, Resilience and Create Happier Individuals"

◆

Acknowledgements

Thanks to all those writers whose work kept me reading from an early age, whose words fired my imagination, and made me want to write my own stories, and whose creative use of language made me aware of the difference between good and bad writing, and of the amazing things that can be done with words – you are a source of ongoing inspiration.

Thanks also to all of the authors that I have worked with in recent years – I am honoured that you have chosen me to coach you, to edit your work, to design and publish your books – thank you for your contributions to the world of inspiring books.

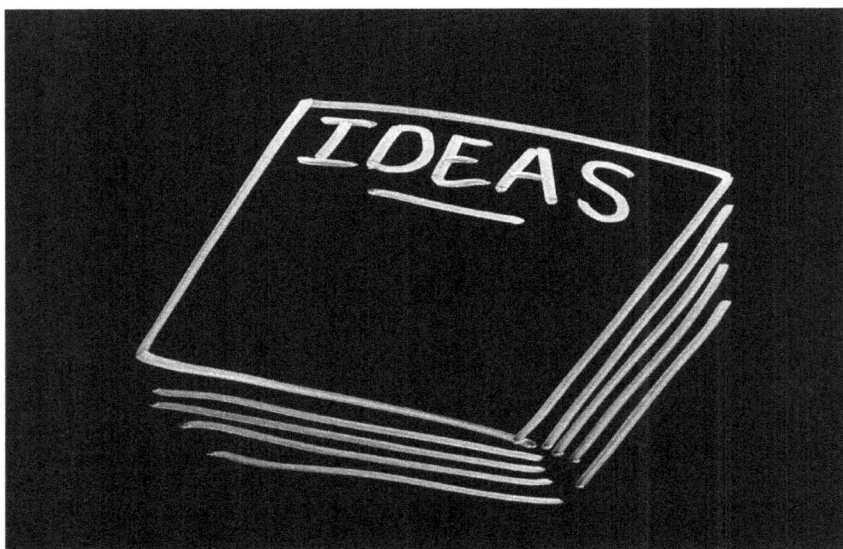

Preface

This book is designed to help you – in the easiest way possible – to improve your writing, to get past your writing challenges, to defeat 'writer's block', or any other issue that is stopping your creative flow. It is presented as a series of short tips, usually one to two pages each, which address various challenges that writers face.

You can read this book in any order that you like – from start to finish, or by browsing through the tips at random, or as a particular challenge hits you. The tips are presented in no specific order, so browse at will. This is designed to be a quick resource for writers at all stages of the process, from first try at writing, through to already having multiple books published.

Each tip addresses a particular issue or concept associated with writing, and with connecting with your readers. Wherever possible, I have noted how the tip applies to both fiction and non-fiction writing. Although a few tips may be specific to one or the other, most apply to both.

Reading these tips should be enjoyable, and will, I hope, enhance your writing skills and get you unblocked from whatever may have been stopping you!

Kim Lambert

2015

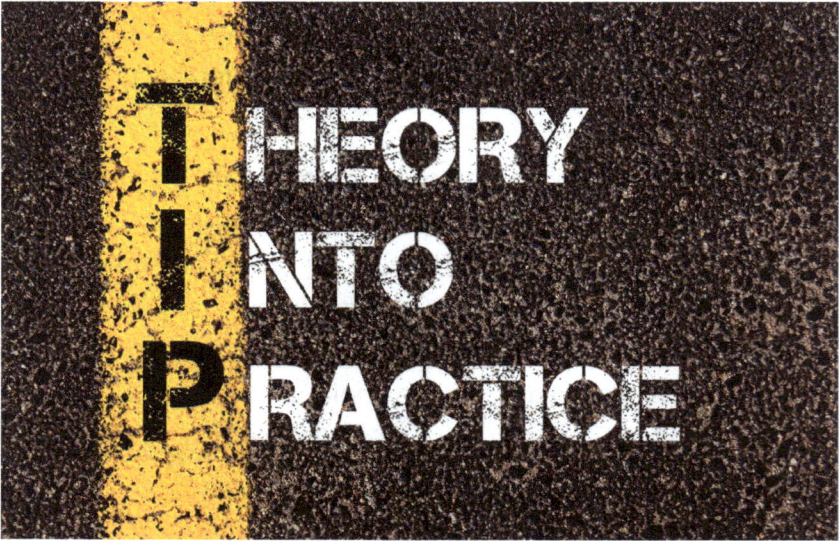

The Tips and Tricks

1.   Know How to Inspire Your Readers

When you write, who do you want to inspire?

What reaction do you want to inspire in them?

If you don't know the answers to those questions, how will you connect with your reader?

How will you know who to market to?

How will you know how to help the right people to find your work?

- Sit with those questions for a while.

- Write some notes to yourself about what you discover.

- Give it 24 hours.

Then reread those notes, then go back and look at your book / posts / whatever you have written so far - does it let you deliver the right results, for the right readers?

Or do you need to rewrite some of it, with them in mind?

2.   Know What Inspires You

What "lights you up" when you talk about it?

You know, the one (or maybe more!) subject that your friends and family say "Nooo, don't ask him / her about that! We'll never shut them up!"

Are you planning to write a book about that?

If you aren't yet, you should be!

The easiest thing to write, is the thing that you care enough about to talk about endlessly. That is also the easiest thing for you to inspire others about!

So, next time someone does ask you about that topic, record what you say, and get it transcribed - you will find that you have a substantial chunk of book right there!

3.   Make Your Characters Real

When you are writing fiction, or telling case studies or other 'personal' stories in non-fiction, there is one key element that it is essential to include.

This is the thing which allows your readers to connect with the characters / people that you are writing about.

It is a remarkably simple thing.

A character must have flaws.

No-one is ever absolutely perfect, so if you write someone as if they are, readers will not be able to connect with them, nor be able to empathize with them.

Show the flaws, the weaknesses and the idiosyncrasies - they will make your characters real.

4. Write in a Way That Will Connect to Those You Want to Inspire

Why do you write?

For many people, the answer is "because I want to inspire others, by sharing my story / what I know".

The next thing that people tell me, though, is "I have no idea how to write, in a way that will do that".

Here is the (multi-part) answer to that.

- You don't have to write a perfect literary masterpiece.

- You do have to care about your words

- You do have to tell your story / explain your knowledge as honestly and authentically as possible.

- You do need to have someone else help you with editing, and coaching you on how to simplify and clarify your writing, so that your meaning is utterly and immediately conveyed to your reader.

- You do need a clear concept of the result that you want for your reader - how will they feel inspired? what will they do as a result of you inspiring them?

- You do need to plan, from the very start, how you will make your writing visible to those who you want to inspire - marketing is necessary - you can't inspire people if they cannot find your work to read it.

- And most importantly of all, you need to truly deeply accept that your story has value, that you are worthy, and that you deserve the recognition and visibility that comes with actually inspiring people. If you write hesitantly, due to not believing that, then you will not inspire, because people will feel that hesitancy in your words.

"Your words are your path to connecting with, and inspiring, others - use the opportunity that writing gives you!"

Kim Lambert

5.   Let Your Readers Live Vicariously

People like living vicariously. That's why they watch reality TV, read biographies, and read magazines about 'real life stories'.

You can use that when you write! Even for non-fiction.

When you write a non-fiction book, about your area of expertise, you should include case studies. Case Studies serve three purposes in your book.

- They illustrate what you are talking about, and make something more real to the reader, through providing an example of how it works.

- They demonstrate your competence - they should be written in such a way that it is clear that the person got the results described because YOU helped them, or because they attended YOUR workshop

- They grab the reader because they are about a real person who is "just like them" getting real results - the reality TV effect!

It is always a good idea to use things in your writing that allow you to connect with people, sell them on your competence, and entertain them too. Especially as it means that you sell your ability to them, your authority increases, and you don't have to be 'salesy' at all to achieve that

6. Getting Your Non-fiction Content Clear

If you are writing a non-fiction book that teaches people how to do something, and are struggling to work out what exactly you need to explain, and how much detail to go into, here is a tip to help you.

If what you are teaching is something that you do in your business, have you ever taught a trainee how to do it? If you have taught someone else, who had no knowledge of it before, then you are well placed to write your book! put your notepad handy, and close your eyes and remember teaching that person.

What did they ask you?

In what order?

How did you answer those questions? Did they understand straight away? Or did you need to rephrase things?

Open your eyes and write down the questions that they asked, in order, and make notes about how you answered and how well they understood.

Now apply that information to the structure of your book, and the level of detail that you go to, in your explanation. If you get stuck again, just repeat the process.

7.   Creating the "Chain of Clues" in Your Non-fiction Book

A good non-fiction book has some things in common with a mystery novel!

At first look, that may seem a bit of a crazy statement, but let me explain.

In a mystery novel, clues are revealed a little at a time, trickled out to you as the story progresses, so that, over the length of the book, you can add up all those little bits of information until you have a clear picture of what is happening.

At the start, you have a vague idea of what may happen, but no idea how you will discover the details. A well written novel then delivers the clues in such a way that the details become clear, seemingly magically, as you read.

A non-fiction book, especially one that sets out to teach the reader something, should be the same.

The reader comes to it with an idea of what they will learn, but no idea of the details of learning, and how to get to that result. The book should deliver pieces of information in each chapter, that are a series of steps (the 'clues') that lead the reader progressively to the point where they know enough to do whatever it is that you are teaching them.

A well written book will make that feel smooth and easy to them - each piece of information will add seamlessly to the previous ones, until, magically, they realize that they now know how to do the thing that the book teaches.

Your reader will enjoy learning, when it happens like this, for exactly the same reason that people enjoy mystery novels - they are exercising their mind, but it is not difficult, they are given the answers, and the mental effort involved in connecting them is enough to make it interesting, but not so much as to make it become "too hard".

When you are planning your non-fiction book structure, try asking yourself "what clues does my reader need, to solve what is, to them, the mystery of how to do this?"

8.   Dealing with Your Emotions When Writing

Whether you write fiction, or non-fiction, there are often things in what you write, which may remind you of events in your past, and bring old emotions to the surface.

Does that worry you? Are you a bit afraid of feeling like that, not sure how to deal with it?

Let's look at that.

There are two possibilities when something rises to the surface like that. One is that it is about things that you have not processed yet, that you have been repressing and hiding. The other is that these are things that you have processed and moved past, but they can still trigger a response when you remember them, because their influence was so strong, for so long.

Either way, having them rise to the surface when you write is a good thing.

If they are unprocessed, now is your chance!

Let yourself feel, explore what you feel, and write about it. What you write in that moment may never end up in your book / blog post etc, but it will allow you to see those feelings in a new light, and give you a chance to move past them.

If they are previously processed things, then breathe, acknowledge the memory, examine the feeling for any new insights it brings, and be grateful that you are past that, but that it has come back to you, now, in this moment, so that you can write with the full depth of feeling that your subject deserves, and create words that others will truly be able to connect to, when they read them.

Emotions are a gift. When we choose to own and acknowledge them, rather than let them own and overwhelm us, they allow us to write in a way that connects completely with our readers.

So, don't fear those moments, even if they sometimes surprise you - embrace and appreciate them!

9.   Getting Richness into Your Descriptions

When you write, because people can't see your face, see you wave your arms around for enthusiasm, or hear your voice tones change, you need another way to let them 'see' and 'feel' your enthusiasm, or the importance of what you are talking about.

This means that the words that you use when you write, even for non-fiction, need to be richer, more dramatic, and more energetic than those that you would use when speaking about the same thing. So food is not just tasty looking, its amazingly rich, succulent, and delicious looking, and has smells that tantalize and draw you in.

You get the idea. You will feel a bit silly writing it to begin with, and it's a fine line between enough rich adjectives to allow the reader to imagine what you want them to, and too many - you do not want overly verbose 'purple prose'. Explore this though, get some friends and family to be test readers, and see what they say.

If the words allow the reader to clearly imagine what you are describing, then with non-fiction they will learn better from you, and enjoy doing so, and with fiction they will feel like they are in your story, not just reading it, and reach the end asking where your next book is, because they don't want the experience to end.

Think about books that you have read recently - how well did they do with this? Did they engage you properly? Or did they fall flat?

10. Getting Unstuck When You are Not Sure What to Write Next

If you are stuck on writing your book (whether fiction or non-fiction), spend some time working on your background notes instead.

Background notes come in two types.

One is the character details and history for fiction, the things that are not told directly in the story, but which cause the characters to act the way that they do.

The other is for both fiction and non-fiction - it is the notes about your target group of readers, detailing what they want to read and why, where they are most likely to hangout online, what other authors' books they read etc etc.

Background notes help you to understand how to structure your book content to best suit your readers, and how to plan your book marketing to reach them.

But, best of all, background notes will often trigger you back into writing your content, because they will give you an insight into what to cover, or how to present it, that you may not have had before.

11. Making Your Writing Easy to Read

Have you noticed how some things that you read just flow along, sliding the information into your head, almost without you noticing, whilst others are painful to read, and leave you with a sense of confusion, or frustration?

Obviously, you want your writing to be in the easy to read category, to leave the reader feeling positive, educated and entertained, and ready to read more from you.

So, how do you do that?

Simple - you plan it. You can write the content in any order that you like, but once it's written, you will need to assemble it into a form that has that flow. So, make a list of the things that you talk about / need to cover in what you have written or plan to write, to get the outcome for the reader that you want to deliver.

Do some things need to be understood before others will make sense? Is there a logical order to the information, which goes from overview and basic concepts about your topic, to more complex aspects, and leads finally to a result, or an ongoing plan?

Move your headings on the list around, until they are in the right order, to create that logical flow, where everything is explained in a way that steadily builds to a final outcome. Now move the pieces of writing around in your Book / document, to put them in that order.

Read through it - do you need to write some extra little linking bits, which help take the reader from one piece of information, smoothly, to the next?

If so, write it, then get someone else to read through the lot, and see how they respond.

If they suggest changes, note those in your plan list, think about them, and only make them if those changes improve the flow.

It's worth taking the time to do this, if it means that the reader loves reading what you write, and comes back for more!

12. Making Things Seem Real to the Reader

If you need to describe an object, or a place, in your writing, and you are struggling to find some words to do it effectively, here is a trick to help you find them.

If it's an object that you have to hand (like a piece of fruit, or something in the house), then go get the object, pick it up, and really LOOK at it. Makes some notes about it based on these questions –

- What shape is it (really, in detail)?

- What color is it?

- Is that color even, or graduated, or blotchy etc?

- What does it smell like? (And is that a nice smell? does the smell remind you of something else? or some place or time else?)

- What does it feel like? Is it hard or soft? Smooth or bumpy? Even or uneven in texture? Does the feeling remind you of any other objects or surfaces?

- What does it taste like (if its edible)

- Does it make any sounds, in any way?

- What is the overall feeling it raises in your mind? Positive? I want to eat it? Negative? Threatening? Comforting?

If it is a place that you need to describe, find a picture of that place (if it's a real place) or of somewhere similar in concept (if it's a made up place) and ask yourself the following questions, while looking at the picture (and write down the exact words that come to your mind in answer):

- What are the main colors in the scene? Are they strong and vibrant, or subtle and almost pastel? Does one color predominate?

- What time of day is it in the picture? Is that the time of day that you need to describe? If not, what would be different at another time of day?

- What smells would you smell, if you were standing in the place pictured? Why would those smells be there? Are they pleasant or unpleasant smells? What would the smells make you want to do? What would the smells remind you of?

- What sounds would you hear, if you were standing in the place pictured? Are they loud or soft? Pleasant or unpleasant? What do those sounds remind you of?

- Would this be a new place for you? And if so, how would you feel because of that?

- Or would it be a familiar place? And how would that make you feel?

- What textures would you be standing on / touching, if you were in the place pictured? What would be under your feet?

- Is the overall feeling of the place good, negative, uncertain, hot, cold etc?

Once you have written yourself notes on your answers to those questions, you will have dozens, if not hundreds of descriptive words and ideas to use in your writing, to truly evoke the thing that you are describing, in the reader's mind.

Good writing transports the reader into what is being described, whether that is a scene in a novel, or a kitchen full of delicious scents and tastes when a recipe is presented.

13.   Understanding What Makes the Structure of a Book Good, or Bad

If you are struggling with working out how you want to structure your book, here is a way to get some ideas.

It's highly likely that you read books in the same genre or topic area as those that you write.

Go to your bookshelf, and pull out the 5 books that you have most liked reading / found most helpful to learn from, in your topic area, and the 5 books that you have found most frustrating to read (no matter how good the actual content is) in that genre.

Sit down and look through them, and make some notes - what is common to all five of the good ones? What is common to all 5 of the bad ones? What does this tell you about what makes a book easy to read and learn from?

Is there something about the way that the good ones are structured that you can apply to your book?

Is there something about the bad ones that makes you want to change how you thought that you would do your book?

14.   Finding the Hidden Books in Your Business, or Your Life

Every so often, revisit the material that you have previously written (regardless of what it was written for at the time), but have not published, or have only made available as bits and pieces, or within a very limited context (like a small workshop).

Look at it with new eyes and ask yourself these questions:

- How many words of content do I have here?

- Is it all on one theme? or is it easily separated into a number of categories?

- How strongly does it relate to the most common problems that I solve for my customers? (or that I talk to people about?)

- Do I immediately see that I can, from where I am now, add new information to it, enhance it in some way?

- You will almost certainly be amazed at how much you have, and at how much you can add to it easily.

- Now consider it as an outline for a series of books :

- What would the series title be?

- What would each book focus on?

- How can you adapt that to best support your current aims, as a business person building authority, or as an author building a following of readers?

Write down your answers to these, and write some notes, then create a plan of action.

It's a lot quicker to release a series of books when you already have most of the content, just hiding there in "all of that old stuff"!!

Being the author of a book gets you respected; being the author of a series takes that to a whole new level.

15. Getting Emotion into Your Writing

For your reader to relate to it, your writing needs to have emotional content - it needs to draw them in, so that they engage with it in some way.

Whilst this is absolutely critical for fiction (or for biography / 'true life stories') it is also true for non-fiction.

Your writing needs character, to present things with a unique and authentic voice. Otherwise, a non-fiction book will become a dry and boring text book.

To achieve emotion in non-fiction, you will need to put yourself into the mind space of your target readers, and understand what they feel about your topic - if they are passionate about it, you will need to be too, if they have a sense of humour, then insert a few slightly funny bits (anything can be funny.....).

Think about why they want to know what you are teaching them - then present your information in a way that engages those feelings.

Dedicated readers will buy every book that you release - because they relate to you, to the way that you explain things, and to the sound of voice that they imagine you to have based on your writing.

16. Use the Fact that People Have Short Attention Spans

People have short attention spans. That is a marvelous thing for a writer !

Why?

Because it means that you do not have to write an enormous book.

A series of smaller books, which address your topic in 'bite sized pieces' will likely sell better, and get you dedicated readers, who come back again and again. (and make you more money in the process!!)

When you go to write, remember that one A4 or letter sized page of typing is equal to 2 pages in a finished paperback or trade paperback sized book.

So, if you can write 50 pages on one aspect of your knowledge, or on 'episode one' of your fiction story, you have a book!

Keep that in mind on days when the task seems overwhelming, and go for a perspective shift.

17.   How to Create Your Chapter Headings

Not sure what to use as your chapter headings?

For non-fiction books, the best chapter headings are questions!

That tells the reader immediately what you are going to tell them – it's about the answer to that question. It makes it easier for you to write too, because you know the answer to the question.

And when a person looks at your book (either physically, or with Amazon's 'look inside' function) they can see the table of contents, and that will immediately show them what you are going to teach them (and lets them see that it will answer *their* questions!), because the Table of Contents is a list of questions (which are your chapter headings).

If you have already written quite a bit, try seeing if you can recast your chapter headings as questions.

Then consider whether the content that you have written answers those questions - you may be surprised at how much more you decide you can write, to really answer those questions!

18.   Getting Unstuck Through Talking

When you are stuck for what to write for a particular chapter in your non-fiction book, or a particular scene in a fiction book, here is a way to get past that.

Get the help of a trusted friend or family member. Get yourself a voice recorder (your phone almost certainly has one on it).

Sit down in a quiet space, hit record, and ask your friend to 'interview you' about the bit you are stuck on.

They should ask general and specific questions all around the topic for non-fiction - whatever they think of, or things that you told them to ask. For fiction, they should ask you about how the various characters feel, what they want, and what they are doing.

Let the conversation wander wherever it goes, just keep talking.

When it winds down naturally, stop.

Get the recording transcribed and read through it.

Pick the bits that are useful, and copy into your main work, and edit.

Or just be inspired by what the conversation uncovered, and start writing, with that as a guide.

19.   Being Aware of the Affect that Your Passion for Your Subject has on Your Writing

When you write, and you are passionate about the things that you write about, it's very easy to become caught up in what you write, and for your fingers to struggle to keep up with your mind.

It is good to get things out of your head and onto the 'page' when you are like that, because your words will be authentic, and the content / what you want to say, will be clearest to you at that point.

But that does not mean that what you write when you are like that will be well written, or actually clearly convey to the reader, what you want to convey to them. In fact, often, if you write like that, then leave it for 24 hours and come back to read it, you will find that its rather jumbled, has missing words, or incomplete sentences, or long tangled rambling sentences - those are all the points where your fingers completely failed to keep up with your mind!

Don't despair! With the clear view that the 24 hours rest has given you, you can adjust it - insert those missing words, ask yourself if you can make any of those sentences shorter (maybe make 2 sentences out of one?), if you can remove any words, and still have the meaning stay clear?

Compact writing, with strong rich words, but not too many at once, has a huge impact. Make sure that each sentence is complete, and does not change tense halfway through.

Look for the statements in your writing that are intended to hit hard to the reader - do they stand out clearly - can you make them stronger and simpler?

After that, do a final spelling and grammar check, look for wrong words (you know, those ones that are a real word, may even sound the same, but are just not the right one for the context that you are using it in).

Then, final check, get someone else to read it - ask them if it reads clearly, makes sense, and what they think your main points are - you may need to do some final adjustment as a result, but you will have a far better piece of writing, and create a far better reader experience, as well as having a much better chance of creating a life changing impact in the readers mind.

20. Writing in 'Bite-sized Pieces'

If the whole concept of writing a book feels like too much, change your perspective

- Can you write an article, about just one small area of what you would like to cover in your book?

- Can you make that between 500 and 1000 words? (That's about 1 to 3 pages of normal typing)

- Can you write one of those, each about a different bit of your topic, every few days?

If you can, and you write between 10 and 20 of them, then you will have a book, of between 60 and 100 pages (10,000 to 20,000 words) in 2 months at worst!

Then you can work with your editor to get them in the right order, and create linking content.

So don't think about that big project, just think about one article at a time, and you will have that book done in no time!

21. Making Your Content Flow

Have you ever read a book that felt sort of 'choppy'?

Where you went from one concept to the next with no smooth transitions, and no idea how that happened?

It's not a very good read, is it?

To get a book to flow, to draw the reader through it smoothly, you will need to write what is called 'linking content'.

That's those bits that make sense of why one bit of information follows the other - it gives the reader clues about what to think about, what ideas to examine closely, in the piece that follows, and how those ideas relate to the piece that they just read.

It is way too easy, as the writer, to forget to write those links - because you know why the bits are related, you understand completely!

 But you are too close to it, and your reader does not know what you know.

Help your reader make those connections - yours will be a better book as a result, and your readers will love you!

22. Overcoming Writers Block – Option 1

So - you decide to sit down and write, you open the document, and..... your mind goes completely and utterly blank.

What do you do now?

If you are writing fiction, ask yourself "What would XXXX (who is a character in your story) do if 'they found a secret door in their house' or 'they discovered that their family had a terrible secret' or 'they discovered that the dog had shredded their favorite chair'?"

It does not matter what the question is and, sometimes, the sillier the better.

The question will get you imagining what they would do - at worst, you will be amused, at best, you will add something to your whole story line, and start writing madly.

The concept here is to see your character in action, so that the rest of their story starts to flow again.

If you are writing Non-fiction, ask yourself "what is the silliest / funniest / weirdest question that anyone has ever asked me about XXXX (where that is your topic area, which your book is about)?"

Write it down - describe the situation, why it was silly / funny / weird, how you answered, and what others could learn from it.

Make some notes about how the question relates to other things that you plan to cover in your book, and if that immediately makes you think of ways to say it, in those chapters, write them now!

Overcoming writers block is like dealing with tasks that seem overwhelming – it's about chopping things into small enough pieces that they seem doable, and picking something easy to start so that you can get some immediate achievements.

So, you need things to think about, and write about, that are not critical, not overwhelming, not "too important to risk getting wrong", but just easy to imagine.

Give this a try next time you are stuck - and see if any really funny or amazing things result!

23. Understanding Outcomes – for You and for Your Reader

There are two key things that you should know, even before you start writing your book.

1. What outcome do you want from the book, for you?

Is the book a chance to help others? Do you want it to drives leads to your business? Do you want it to increase your visible authority in your field, and maybe lead to interviews and speaking engagements? Or do you want it to create a steady stream of passive income? Or is it a combination of those?

2. What outcome do you want from the book, for the reader?

Should they come out of reading it having learnt something specific? With an action plan? Wanting the next book in the series? Wanting to work with you, one on one? Wanting to be a customer of your business? Wanting to refer their friends to your book, and your business? Or something else again?

The answers to those two things will determine how you structure your book, and the feel and style of your writing, and presentation.

As a business owner, when you write a book on a topic related to your business, the whole book is, effectively, a long form sales letter, from start to finish - so structuring it with the same things in mind, that copywriters consider for a sales letter, is very important, to help you decide just how to present things.

For your reader, you knowing what outcome you want for them is critical – if you do, you can structure the book to deliver it, and give them a sense of completion, of satisfaction and satisfied readers come back for you next book.

If you don't know, then you have no hope of giving them that outcome – and unsatisfied readers not only don't come back, but they tend to write bad reviews!

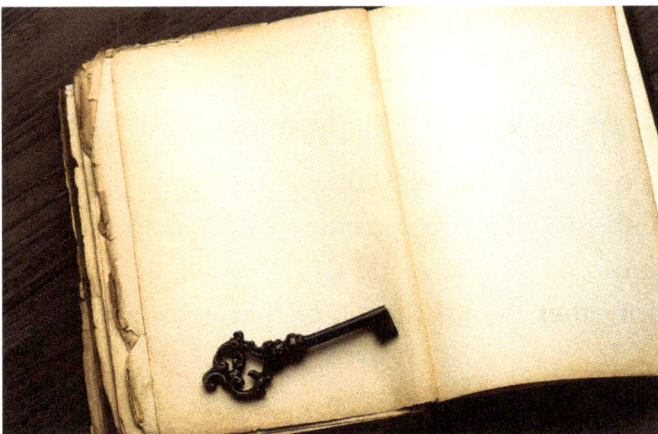

24.   Why You Need Background Notes

When writing fiction, you, as the author, will know all sorts of things about your characters' lives, that may never surface in your story, or may not become visible to the reader for a long time, yet they shape how the characters act.

So, to make sure that you keep that stuff straight, without revealing it before due time, you need a set of notes (that may end up as big as your actual book!) where you write dot point details, or whole narratives, of what happened in the characters' life, what made them think and act the way that they do. This should be quite analytical - keep the emotion for writing the story itself.

You will also need a genealogy for your characters, and research notes about locations that you intend to set parts of your story in.

Creating all of that can be as much fun as creating the story itself, and will make the writing of the story immensely easier.

And, if you make it a series, you will just keep growing that solid background to write in the context of. And, if your series does well, you can do a "The World Of……" book, or a prequel, or any number of other things with all of that extra material you have created!

25. Writing Clear Instructions

If you struggle to explain things clearly in your writing (especially for non-fiction books, or business instructions etc), because you know the thing that you are trying to explain too well, here is a trick to make that easier.

If you want to explain how to do a task, the simplest way to capture it is to show someone else. Ideally, use a screen capture video making tool, like Camtasia, or, for an outdoor or physical task, get someone to video you, and record it as you go. Start the recording, and do the task, telling the person beside you what you are doing, every step of the way, and make sure that they ask you questions as you go, if they think that anything you say is not clear enough.

When you are done, you can play the video back to yourself as you write the instructions for your book, thus making sure that you don't miss any steps (you know, the ones that seem blindingly obvious to you, because you know it so well, but may not be obvious to someone who has never done the task before).

If you really want to take the lazy approach, you can even get someone to transcribe what is said in your recording, so that all you have to do is final edit the result.

26. Why the Way That You use Vocabulary in Your Writing Matters

As we grow up (or spend more time using the language, if it is our second language) we learn more words. Our vocabulary expands. We each learn different words.

There are some core ones - apparently, you only need to know about 1500 words to operate completely effectively in English! But there are thousands and thousands of other words.

Consider the major English dictionaries - they have an enormous number of words defined.

So - why do we learn some words, and not others? We learn words for a few reasons:

- Because our parents and family members use those words in talking to us, or in our presence
- Because we study a topic, or work in a particular area, and learn all of the words associated with that topic or job
- Because we love to read about a particular topic, or period in history, and we learn from the words used in the books
- Because words fascinate us, and we go looking for new ones to learn.

Generally, the more chance a person has for education (whether formally at school or University, or informally, by having access to, and an interest in, lots of books and information on a topic), the more words they will learn, and the more complex words they will come to know.

So people at different socio economic levels will know different words, and people working in different job 'families' will know different words.

What does that mean for you, as a writer?

If you write non-fiction, it means that you need to understand what socio economic group your primary reader audience are from, and choose your words to suit them. You may also need to learn some specialised words, which are only used in the context of your topic, and make sure that you use them correctly.

If you write fiction, it is rather more interesting!

As a fiction writer, you are putting words in the mouths of your characters. Generally, in any story, there will be characters from different backgrounds, education levels, and jobs, and those aspects of the characters will be part of what drives your storyline. For your reader to find your characters believable, to relate to them, and connect with them, you will need to make each character use the right kind of words, in the right way, to fit their background.

Where this becomes challenging, is not just where the character has less education and experience than you, so you have to 'repress' your own vocabulary to write them, but when the character has more education than you and / or works in a very specialised area, that you don't work in. The only way to write that character is for you to learn new words, to learn about their specialisation, and all of the words that come just with that topic area.

So, set aside time for that sort of research, when planning your writing program. You will learn some fascinating things, and meet some amazing people, when you step out there and ask someone to help you write convincingly about their field.

Enjoy doing this – it's worth it. Why? because a novel in which characters definitely have unique and appropriate ways of speaking, relevant to who they are in the world, will immediately feel more real to the reader (even if they don't know why) and the reader will enjoy your book more, be more likely to give you a good review, and be more likely to tell their friends about your book.

So - write better, learn more words, and meet more people - what's not to like?

27.   Choosing What to Write

When you decide to write about the topic you know best, it usually hard to start

Why?

Because you know too much!

To stop the overwhelm, start by writing down the ten things that your clients, or the people you discuss things with, most commonly ask you about, related to your topic.

Once you have that, you have what could be the chapter headings for a book - because, if that's what people ask you, that is also what people will search for, when looking for a book in your topic area.

You may even be lucky enough to find that each common question has enough content in the answer to be a separate book – there you go, you've got a series!

28. The Concept of "Less is More"

Think about what happens when you buy a book yourself. Books with a good layout, with plenty of illustrations (for non-fiction) to break up the big blocks of text, and with a good amount of 'white space' around the text, so that it is easy to read, and is 'packaged' in easily 'digestible' chunks are easier to learn from, easier to read (especially if you only have short bits of time to read in) and a better reader experience than books that are 'textbook like' monsters of dense text.

When you make your book with that sort of spacious and easy to read layout, you end up with more pages of book, for the same number of words....

When we sit down to write, we want to tell the world everything that we know on our subject of expertise, or we want to tell them all of our amazing fiction story as soon as possible.

But doing that is counterproductive.

Why? Because breaking it up into multiple, medium sized (100 pages or so, at paperback size) books produces the following positive results:

- Better reader experience, because it's well laid out and easy to read and learn from

- You get greater respect and authority as an author, because you have written not just one book, but a series

- You earn more money! People will pay only so much for a single book, no matter how big it is, but they will happily pay a good rate for each smaller book.

- You can space out the release of your books over time - this makes it easier for you to get them written, gets the readers really wanting your next book, and, at the same time, does not overwhelm the reader with too much info at once.

So – **'Less is More'** - less info, delivered in a better way, gets a better result, than drowning the reader in a deluge of content, all at once.

Look at your current writing projects and consider this - how can you use this concept to get a better result, for you, and your reader? (And work less hard in the process!)

29.   Finding Your Plot Line

Do you know what sort of stories you want to write? (Like romance, fantasy, horror etc?) Yet you can't think of a story line?

If so, then think about a setting (what town, place, world etc?) and three characters - the hero / heroine, the 'bad guy' (the person who is the threat or conflict generator) and the hero / heroine's lover/ friend/ supporter. Give them names, and a few physical or habitual characteristics.

Choose one dramatic thing to happen - like an argument, love scene, kidnapping - whatever.

Write that scene.

Then work out how they got there, and what happens after.

A story is basically

- Introduce the characters / drama,
- Show a small conflict,
- Resolve it,
- Have a bigger conflict or threat happen,
- Have heroics resolve that,
- Have a conclusion (which may be a 'cliffhanger' to lead to your next story....)

If you have the key pieces for each step, you can fill in the blanks in between!

30. Creating Reality Through Significant Life Events

When you write, (for fiction) make sure that your characters have birthdays, anniversaries, and other 'important life events' - choose dates etc, and capture that in your backstory notes.

Make those events happen in your story, let them affect the flow of events - real people have life events, and stuff happens on those days! Doing this will make your characters more relatable to, more real to the reader. And, it will provide you with an excuse for all sorts of conflicts and interactions.

For non-fiction - if your topic is about something where you can relate it to life events, do.

For example - if it's a cookbook, suggest some recipes that are good for birthday dinners. If it's a book on positive thinking, suggest some affirmations for birthdays, which are about the good aspects of getting older!

You can make your knowledge, and what you are teaching, more accessible to the reader if you give them practical ways to use it in their real life, with really specific suggestions.

Go back and look at what you have written - can you enhance it with a little bit of 'life connection'?

31.   Start with the Senses.

What does that mean?

The very first sentence / paragraph of a book, article or blog post should engage the reader fast. The best way to do that is to draw them into whatever you are talking about / telling in such a way that they can imagine themselves there / imagine tasting the cakes that the recipes are for / imagine the smells on a sun-baked beach / imagine the sounds in a secluded bush retreat / imagine the feel of the sand between their toes...... etc etc

How do you do that?

You use evocative adjectives, which are specifically about sight, sound, taste, touch and smell.

So not

"She stood on the beach and looked out to sea"

but

"She felt the soft white sand shift between her toes as she stood on the deserted beach, with only the sound of the waves and the cry of the seagulls for company. The summer sun baked her skin and the salt smell of the sea reminded her of other days, other beaches, and she stared out to sea, lost in memories".

The second version is full of words that relate to the senses, that make it very easy for the reader to empathise with the character, to imagine themselves there, on the beach, to remember their own beach moments, and to want to know what happens next, because they are, in that moment, being the character that you have written.

Even for non-fiction, this is important - if you tell them that the recipe is tasty, they imagine it, if you tell them that doing that exercise will feel good, and describe glowing health and strength, they connect with it.

Next time you write, stop after a while, and look at the words that you have used - can you make the richer? Can you add or change things to engage the senses of your readers?

Play with the idea - you will find that your writing improves, and that readers want more.

32.   Creating a Good Reader Experience

What makes a good reader experience? Why does understanding that matter, when it comes to getting yourself going, writing that book / blog post / article etc?

Let's start with your own experiences as a reader. What makes a book more easily readable for you? Think of books that you have read, which you became totally absorbed in, and enjoyed / easily learnt from, so much so that you barely noticed that you were reading - the information just rolled in to your brain.

Find one or two of those books again, and look at them. Really look.

What is their layout like? Are there pictures and diagrams? Is there white space around the text, to make it easy on the eye? Is it a good font? Is the content well edited, with no spelling mistakes or odd grammar? Are the diagrams clear and easy to understand? What else about it makes that book better to read than others?

Now consider the book that you are writing - what can you do, in how you word things, in how you explain things, in how you lay things out on the page, that will make your book emulate those books that were good to read? What about those books would you like your book to emulate? Do you admire any of those good to read books for more than just ease of reading?

What is it, about the content, and how it is delivered, that makes you admire those books?

Those things are what makes a good reader experience - if you consciously seek to make your writing deliver those things, then your book will deliver a good reader experience (with the collaboration of your editor and formatter, who will make sure that the layout concepts work, and support the reader experience that you are aiming for).

If you are stuck with writing your book, read back through what you have written so far, and pretend that you have never seen it before - how does the reader experience feel? As the reader, what do you want to know next? What do you feel is missing?

Now write those missing / next bits.

Always consider the reader, and what outcome you want for them, as a result of them reading your book.

33.   How Much Should I Write?

This is a common question - most people have no idea how many words fit on an A4 or Letter sized page, or a paperback book sized page, and no idea how many words makes a good blog post, article, non-fiction book or fiction book. So, here is some information for you, to help you get a feel for how much you need to write, to get the result that you want.

It's less than you think!

- A good blog post will be anywhere between 300 and 2000 words, depending on your topic area and style.

- A good article can be as short as 150 words for some magazines, and even a feature article is rarely more than 2000 words!

- A well laid-out, with pictures / diagrams, non-fiction book, of approx. 100 pages, is only 10,000 to 12,000 words.

- A short non-fiction book, done to use as a lead magnet for your business, can be as little as 3,000 words, fleshed out will pictures.

- A short story can be as little as 1500 to 3000 words

- Many published shorts stories and novellas are under 10,000 words

- A longish novel will be around 60,000 words (that's about 200 pages or more!)

- A very big non-fiction book (or a compendium of three or four non-fiction books published as a bundle) will still only be approx. 45,000 words, even though it may be 300 pages or more.

Looking at that, does it start to seem easier to get there?

One A4 or Letter page (the default page size in Microsoft Word) is approx. 300 words, at 12 point text (most fonts – some will vary).

Most people can write between 300 and 1500 words an hour, if they keep focussed on the writing.

So, don't feel like you have to write an encyclopaedia worth of text, before you will be ready to publish - readers want quick, easily digestible information, delivered in neat bundles.

Now, reassess what you have already written - is your first book already done? And you didn't even realise?

34.   Research the Small Stuff!

What does that mean? Details are what creates the 'world of the book' in the readers mind (fiction) or gives your words authority (non-fiction).

If you are reading a novel, where people ride horses, and you, a horse person, know that all of the terminology used is wrong, then it breaks you out of the story, instantly - no matter how good the writing is, overall, the immersion in the story will be spoilt for you, because the wrong terminology will jar.

This is equally true if the novel is set in a historical time period, and the words used for things are modern ones, or the descriptions of clothes, social behaviour and settings etc are not correct for the period - someone who loves that period, and has learnt lots about it (who would, in theory be your ideal reader) is lost to you, because you did not do enough research to get it right.

For non-fiction, be that a 'teaching book' or a memoir or similar, the same applies - get your settings right, get the chronology of things in a memoir right, check the scientific truth of anything that you state or quote - nothing draws the picky haters faster than stating a scientific untruth.

Detailed research may seem tedious, but it pays off handsomely.

If you get it right, your readers love you, they buy your next book on pre-order, and they tell their friends - "here is an author who can finally get XXXXX right".

An additional bonus will be how much you, personally, learn.

You will discover things that you have never imagined, you will have a source of trivia for conversation forever, and, the more that you learn about your chosen topic area or period, the easier each successive story or book will be, to get right, to make it addictive to readers, because they will have an amazing immersive experience when they read your work.

Go to your book collection. Find a novel that you love, and one that you really struggled to finish, if you did at all. Re-read parts of them - preferably parts where settings, tools, clothes or activities are described - you will almost certainly find that, in the book that you did not like, there are all sorts of little details that are either 'just wrong' or seem odd, or are incorrect, and about a topic that is a hobby or interest of yours.

Start to look for this sort of thing, in everything that you read, and learn from it - get better at research, and at understand what sort of details make a book 'real' to a reader.

35.   Revisit Your Life for Clarity.

If you are trying to explain, in your writing, how to do something, and you are not sure if what you have written is clear enough, revisit your personal experience, when you first learned how to do what you are explaining.

Close your eyes and remember, as clearly as you can, what happened when you were first shown that task - what questions did you ask? What bits of it challenged you most? What took longest to stick in your mind?

Then open your eyes and review what you have written - does it answer those questions? Does it break down the challenging bits as much as possible? Does it cover the hard to remember bits specifically?

Adjust what you have written, to make sure that, had you had those instructions when you learnt it, learning would have been much easier.

The same concept can be applied in fiction too - if what you are describing is a character's first experience - of a place, an emotion, and activity - then revisit your first experience of that, and really remember the sights, sounds, smells, tastes, textures and bodily reactions that were part of that first experience for you, then describe them in as much detail as possible, with lots of strong descriptive words.

Doing this regularly will ensure that your writing stays accessible to your readers, is easily empathized with, and makes them want to read more, because they have connected with what you have written so strongly.

36.   Getting Dialogue and Conversational Writing Right

In books that are either fiction, where you have dialogue between characters, or non-fiction where you may quote people speaking, how do you make the dialogue feel natural, and read in such a way that it 'sounds' in the readers head, just as if the character is speaking to them?

If you are telling your story in a book, how do you make it read as if you are personally speaking to the reader?

When we speak to a person right in front of us, we use a sort of 'shorthand' - we contract words, we leave some words out, we let our tone of voice and body language create the clarity of what we mean, in conjunction with our words. When we write, we need to use, usually, uncontracted words (do not, rather than don't), and add back in the missing words (such as that, to and of) and use punctuation to indicate where the breathing pauses go, so that the reader reads it with the meaning clear to them.

When we write dialogue, we have to balance those two approaches. Contracted words in dialogue will make it seem more natural. Sentence structure may be different, if the speaker of the dialogue is of a particular language or cultural background - we must think about how our character would speak, which is quite likely to be rather different from how we, personally, speak.

We need enough punctuation to make things read correctly, without making the feel of the dialogue stilted.

If you are writing a non-fiction book, where you are teaching the reader, in a very 'person to person' style, you have a similar challenge. You need to balance contractions and punctuation, and use of colloquial words, to create a personal feel, which has your unique voice, yet is still clearly understandable to the reader. Always get someone else to read your draft and ask them if it feels personal, or stilted - then adjust.

Particularly for fiction, where there is a lot of dialogue, it is good to make the non-dialogue parts of the writing more 'formal' in style and structure, so that the casual 'reality' of the dialogue stands out by comparison, and makes the characters more real and relatable as a result.

So - dialogue, or 'personal voice' contains more contracted words, less punctuation, more colloquial words and more culturally specific terms

Description, or general text contains more punctuation, less contracted words, less colloquial or culturally specific words and has a more formal feel overall.

37.   Who Will Read Your Book? Who Are You Writing For?

The first answer that people tend to give, to those questions, is "anyone who is interested". If that was your answer too, then you are creating a problem for yourself.

There are thousands of genres of books (both fiction and non-fiction), and each person will only be interested in reading some of them.   If, in your writing, you try to please everyone, your writing will lack intensity, and will engage no-one. Additionally, you can't market to everyone - marketing needs to be specific to a topic area to get people's attention.

So, how do you work out who your audience are? (Because you will need to do so, to both make your writing easier, and to make it possible for you to tell that audience about your book once it is published.)

Start by looking at the key points of your story - what are you writing about? Let's say you are writing a romance novel - that sounds straight forward, doesn't it? It's not. Romance, as a genre, can cover everything from pretty hard core erotica with some love story thrown in, all the way through to Christian romance stories with not even a hint of a sexual thought. It can be set anywhere in history, now or the future, and anywhere in the world or beyond. Someone who likes reading stories at one end of that spectrum, is not going to buy a book with content at the other end.

So, if you want your book to sell, you need to understand who will read it - what is that person like, what do you need to put in your book (or not put in your book) to make it fit the pattern of what they want to buy? Create notes about your ideal buyer and reader audience and keep them handy.

If you are writing, and are unsure about exactly what to do with a bit of your plot, or how your characters will act, or exactly how extreme you will make a situation or emotion in the story, pull out those notes and ask yourself "What would this person prefer to read here? What would they expect the character to do?" You will instantly get a feel for how to solve your problem.

For nonfiction, the concept is the same - do not clutter up your book with too many topic areas or ideas - keep it simple and aimed at one target buyer. If you have lots of material across a range of areas, don't jam it all into one book - rejoice, you have the material for a series, which will mean more authority and more cash flow for you, and happier readers as well.

Now, go back and review what you have written (both finished and unfinished) and consider it with this in mind - have you targeted your reader well, or not?

38. What Makes People Feel Inspired by What You Write?

So - you want to write a book that inspires others, that changes lives, but you have no idea how to write words that will connect with the reader that strongly. Let's look at what makes people feel connection, when they read.

There are a few key things that allow something written to have a real impact. They are:

- The reader feels like you are talking just to them, like you can magically see inside what they are thinking.

- The 'case studies' or examples that you give present real people that the reader feels are 'just like them, or someone that they know'.

- The reader feels like the information or story that they read talks about something that touches on the major emotions - love, grief, fear and anger, overcoming adversity etc, so that they live the story vicariously.

So - how do you make your writing do that?

Start by understanding that people are 95% the same, and only 5% unique - that 95% similarity is what lets science study the psychology of why we do things, and understand what triggers reactions in people.

So while each person's individual story will be different in the detail (that's that 5% uniqueness) there will be common themes, and common types of reactions to events.

Do some study - do some reading about human psychology around the topic area that your book is about. That will let you get some understanding of how your likely readers may feel, of what they may desperately want in their lives, but be afraid to go for.

And knowing that, you start to know what to talk about to inspire them.

To inspire someone, you do not need to know the details of their individual story, you just need to know the general things that are most likely to be true, if they are facing the problem that you are addressing.

So, if your book aims to inspire women who are rebuilding their lives after a disastrous relationship, you don't need to know exactly what happened to them, but you do need to know that research indicates that most of them will be suffering a significant lack of self-confidence, a lack of self-worth, fear of how they will support themselves (financially and emotionally), and fear that future relationships will turn out "just the same".

With that information, you can choose what you say, how you say it, and what examples you use, to be certain that your target readers will be able to feel those three things that I mentioned above.

If you have clients now, that you help with the issues that your book addresses, then take notes for yourself, about what things, that you say to them in coaching sessions, most often cause them to tell you that it's an 'aha' moment for them, or that what you said last session has had a profound effect on them since.

Because those things should go in your book - you already know that they inspire people and get results!

When you work with a coaching client, you almost certainly can work things out, about what they feel and what they need to hear, even if they don't feel able to tell you the deep details of what is going on for them.

That is exactly what you need to do for your readers - provide content that most people (who are in your target audience) are likely to respond and relate to.

When you discuss things, make sure that you use lots of descriptive and emotion laden words - you want people to solidly empathise and connect, before you then talk about, usually in less intense words, the things that they can do to change.

Then go back to more intense descriptive and emotional words when you talk about the benefits, the amazing and positive things that they will achieve by changing.

The key to inspiration is NOT being specific - be general enough for any reader to relate to, and emotional enough to connect.

Have fun listening to yourself, when you write, and speak, and really hearing peoples responses - you already know how to inspire, you just need to write it down.....

39.   Get Some Humour Into It !

No matter how serious the post, article or book you are writing, having a few lighter moments in it will engage your readers more.

Why?

Because people tend to have a strong sense of humour, even in the darkest parts of life - we make jokes when we feel desperate and depressed, to try to make light of it, to cheer ourselves up.

We see humour in bad situations - we even have a term for it - "black comedy". So, if you can lighten your work here and there, people relate to that - it's a part of what most people do themselves, creating that touch of humour in any situation.

Be careful with that humour though - if possible, make any funny stories be about you, or about someone else in a way that is very positive - do not present something that could be seen as "laughing at those less well off than yourself" or "making others 'stupid' ".

You want to seem warm, friendly and happily caring. Or your characters need to be like that, in your novel (unless, of course, it's the dark, sarcastic villain talking....).

In non-fiction books, humour can often be achieved by including a few cartoons in the illustrations in your book - things that take a humorous look at the topic you are discussing.

Or use yourself as a case study (especially if your book is a result of your personal journey) - tell that story, about the incident that was absolutely horrible at the time, but which is, in hindsight, rather funny (especially if, as a result, amazing good things happened, that you could not even imagine when in the middle of it).

You don't have to tell jokes to be funny, and you don't need to mock others to be funny - just add a slight touch of humour here and there, and others will see you (or your characters) as real, as people that they can relate too, and will love your work as a result.

Go back and have a look at the posts or articles that you have written in the past, that got the most positive reader reactions - how many of them have a touch of humour in there? Can you use this approach in future? Do some funny stories come to mind as you read this?

40.   Overcoming Writers Block – Option 2

If you sit down to write, and your mind instantly goes blank, and the words refuse to come, it's not that you are 'hopeless at writing' or any of those other thoughts that may chase through your mind.....   It is likely something much, much simpler.

It is because you don't know enough yet, about the next piece that you have to write.

Think about that for a minute.

If you are writing non-fiction, it means that you can't explain it, in words, because you are not clear enough in your mind on exactly what it is / how you do it, so you can't explain it to someone else.

So, instead of sitting there, beating yourself up for not writing, get up, and go and do whatever it is that you are trying to explain - but do it mindfully - take physical or mental notes of every step of what you do, then come back and have another go at writing that bit of your book.

If you are writing fiction, it means that you are not clear enough on either your plot line (just exactly why is this scene in the book? Where is it taking the characters???), or on the personal characteristics of your characters (you know what action needs to happen in the scene, but you have no idea of how your character would react to that action, or why they would react that way).

If you don't know for sure where the plot is going, work on that - write notes, think about all the options - what paths can the story take, and still get to the desired final end? Note them down, and mentally explore them - does one resonate more than the others? Does one feel like it would be easier to write than the others? If it does, go with that.

If the problem is the characters' reactions, again, don't sit there beating yourself up. Work on your backstory notes - work out how that character would react, and why - what has happened in their past, to make them respond that way. Write down your decisions about their life history and reactions - you will find it incredibly useful later!

Once you start writing notes about these things, you will find that you can start writing the actual story again, because the context will get clear in the back of your brain, and you will have no doubts about what is going to happen.

Don't be surprised if this way of unblocking yourself causes a change of direction or structure in your book - it will almost certainly be better for it!

41.   Your Reader Does Not Know What You Know!

Always remember that your reader does not know what you know - that's why they want to read your book!

Whether its fiction (you know the backstory and the secrets, they can't wait to discover them as the story unfolds) or non-fiction (they want to learn from you, to get the information that only you have that will solve their problem for them) the key is that you, as the author, know more than your reader.

And that means that you can't make any assumptions about what their baseline knowledge is.

So, when you write, spell out the detail clearly (unless of course, in your fiction, it's not yet time to reveal that thing....).

What seems blindingly obvious to you, because you know it so well, will not necessarily be obvious at all to your reader.

42. Make Your Writing Clear, Even When Daily Life is Crazy

Daily life is full of lots and lots of little tasks. None of them are exactly difficult, most of them don't take very long to do at all. But..... when you add them all up, suddenly the day is gone, or you wonder what you did, because you can't remember, yet you are exhausted.

When you write, whether fiction or non-fiction, you need to keep it clear and simple, or your reader will feel like you do, at the end of the day, when they get to the end of the book.

For fiction, that means concentrating only on the key scenes and actions, and not "over detailing" - you don't need to describe every character in a scene in excruciating detail - a passing comment about someone wearing "their usual blue tones" or similar will make them real, without swamping the reader in detail.

You also don't need to tell the life of the characters in minute by minute detail (or the book will never end!) - you only need to tell the key scenes, the ones that are 'tipping points' for the action, that are critical for the reader to see, to move the story along. Everything else can be covered by passing mention in one of those scenes, or implied, not shown. The only time that the crazy detail should be in your fiction, is if you are describing a character having a day like that - where you want the reader to feel the chaos with them.

For non-fiction, that means recognising when short simple sentences, and very plain instructions and supporting information, are enough - it's the balance between providing the information that is needed, and creating a boring textbook of all known info on the topic!

No one enjoys reading heavy academic style textbook like works, with huge blocks of solid text and complex language (unless they are studying that topic and MUST read it!). Make your non-fiction book easy to read, open and inviting, and clean and simple to understand. All that extra detail - keep it for the next book in your series......

Next time you write, review your first draft, and ask yourself

> "Does this need to be in here? Have I gone into unnecessary detail? What can I take out, without changing the meaning?"

You may be surprised at how much you can simplify it, and how much clearer, and more impactful, it becomes in the process.

End Note

I hope that you have enjoyed these tips, and found them useful in your writing. I would love to hear from you (you can find my social media links on the next pages) – please let me know how these tips have helped you, and what you would like to see in my future books.

There is so much that can be written, about writing!

WRITE WELL !

WRITE OFTEN !

TO YOUR WRITING SUCCESS !

ABOUT THE AUTHOR

Kim Lambert is an 8 times Amazon Bestselling Author, Motivational Speaker, Photographer, Writing and Publishing Coach, and a Travel Writer, with more than 10 books published to date. (Find her on Amazon at http://www.amazon.com/Kim-Lambert/e/B00I8KGK4Y/)

She is also the owner of a publishing company (http://www.dreamstonepublishing.com) which publishes books for a variety of authors, and also works with other large publishing companies to enhance and update their current catalogues for digital book delivery.

Kim is the creator of the Product Creation Launchpad course (http://www.productcreationlaunchpad.com/pclsp) and the Zero to Book 3 day writing course.

She is Managing Editor of Life Grow Change – the Magazine. (http://www.livegrowchange.guru)

She lives near Canberra, Australia, and travels as often as possible.

You can connect with Kim on Social media at

https://au.linkedin.com/in/kimlambertpublisher ☐

https://www.facebook.com/DreamstonePublishing

and

https://www.facebook.com/groups/WritersCollaboratingAndLearningForSuccess/

https://twitter.com/DreamstoneBooks

https://plus.google.com/+Dreamstonepublishing/posts

and

https://plus.google.com/+DreamstonepublishingWritersCommunity/posts

https://www.pinterest.com/kimlambert1/

@DreamstoneBooks

Other Books from Dreamstone Publishing

Dreamstone publishes books in a wide variety of categories – here are some of our other books:-

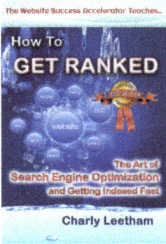

Get Ranked
- The Art of Search Engine Optimisation and Getting Indexed Fast
(The Website Success Accelerator Teaches....)

By Charly Leetham

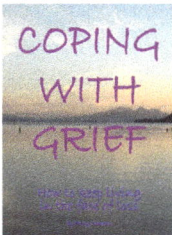

Coping With Grief

By Penny Clements

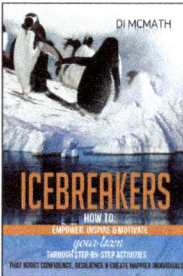

"Icebreakers : How to Empower, Motivate and Inspire Your Team, Through Step-by-Step Activities That Boost Confidence, Resilience and Create Happier Individuals"

By Di McMath

All Books available from all Amazon sites and other book stores, and available for Kindle too!

The Father Balance
How YOU, as a Father, can successfully build a career and, at the same time, still keep your marriage and family together !

By Leith Adams

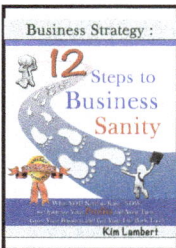

Business Strategy :
12 Steps to Business Sanity
How to Optimize Your Profits and Your Time, Grow Your Business and Get Your Life Back Too!

By Kim Lambert

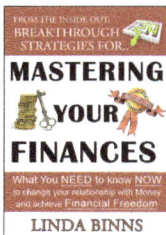

From The Inside Out:
Breakthrough Strategies for Mastering Your Finances:
What YOU Need to Know NOW to Change Your Relationship with Money and Achieve Financial Freedom

By Linda Binns

Want to know when our next books are coming out ?

Be first to get all the news – sign up for our newsletter at

http://www.dreamstonepublishing.com